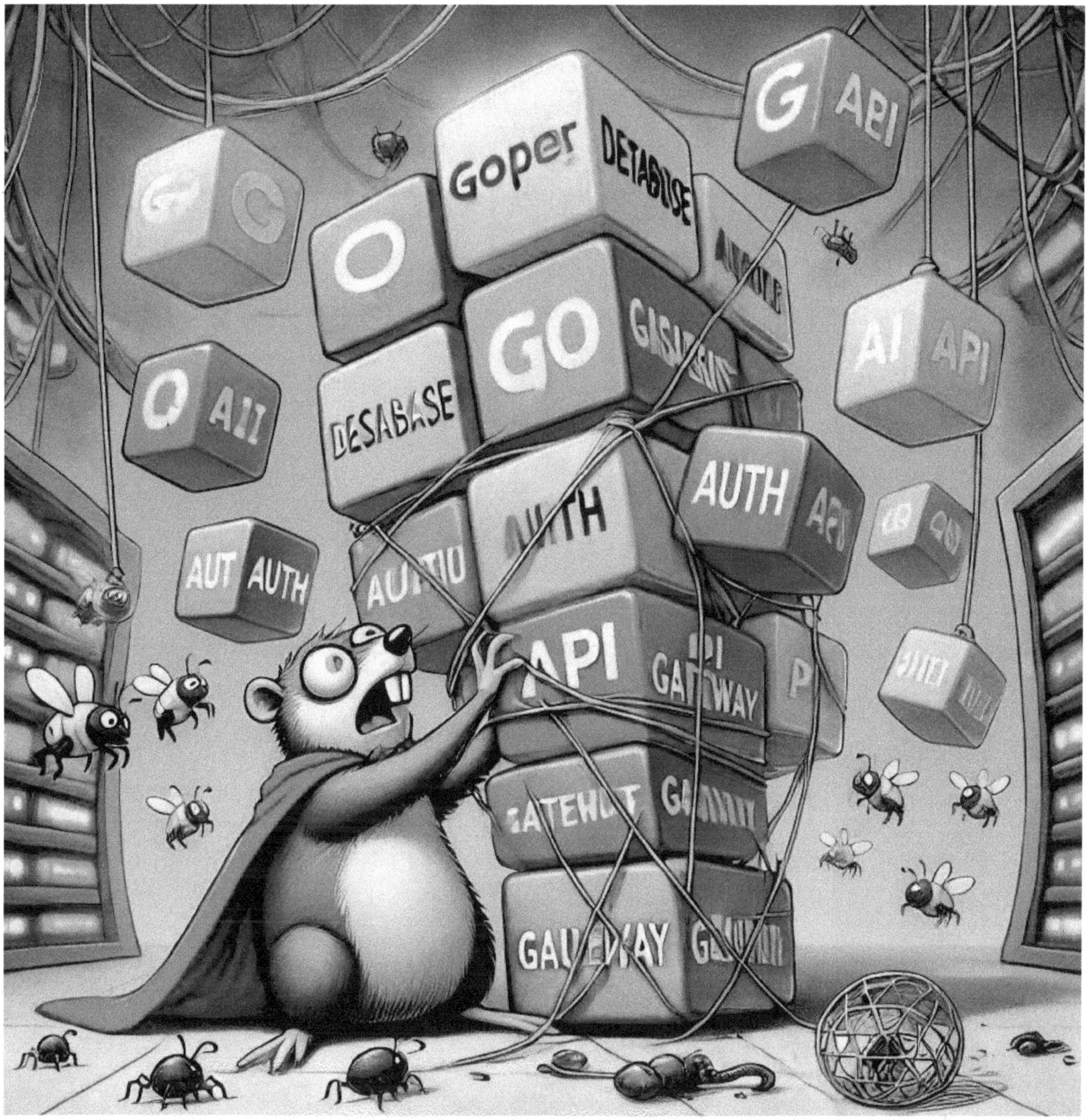
Goper
GO
DESABASE
AUTH
API
AI
AUT

Go Big or Go Home: Building API Services with GoLang

(And Laughing Along the Way)

CHAPTER 1 : Hello, World! Or Should I Say, Hello, Panic?

Setting up your Go environment and cloning the go-api-service repository. A step-by-step guide to getting your project off the ground without setting your laptop on fire.

1. Download and Install Go

Windows:

1. **Download the Installer**

   Visit the official Go website (https://golang.org/dl/) and download the Windows `.msi` installer.

2. **Run the Installer**

   Double-click the `.msi` file and follow the prompts. The installer automatically sets up the necessary environment variables.

3. **Verify Installation**

   Open the Command Prompt or PowerShell and run:
   ```
   go version
   ```

   You should see the installed version of Go.

macOS:

1. **Download the Installer**

   Download the macOS `.pkg` file from the official Go website (https://golang.org/dl/).

2. **Run the Installer**

   Open the `.pkg` file and follow the installation prompts.

3. **Verify Installation**

   Open the terminal and run:
   ```
   go version
   ```

   The installed version of Go should be displayed.

Linux:

1. **Download the tarball**

   Visit the <u>Go download page</u> (https://golang.org/dl/) and download the appropriate
   `.tar.gz` file for your architecture.

   Example command for downloading Go 1.20.6 (replace the version as needed):
   ```
   wget https://go.dev/dl/go1.20.6.linux-amd64.tar.gz
   ```

2. **Extract and Install**

   Remove any previous Go installation:
   ```
   sudo rm -rf /usr/local/go
   ```

   Extract the tarball to `/usr/local`:
   ```
   sudo tar -C /usr/local -xzf go1.20.6.linux-amd64.tar.gz
   ```

3. **Set Environment Variables**

   Add the Go binary path to your shell profile (`~/.bashrc`, `~/.zshrc`, or equivalent):
   ```
   export PATH=$PATH:/usr/local/go/bin
   ```

   Apply the changes:
   ```
   source ~/.bashrc
   ```

4. **Verify Installation**

   Check the installed version:
   ```
   go version
   ```

---

2. Set Up a Workspace

1. **Create a Go Workspace**

   By default, Go uses the `~/go` directory as the workspace. You can change it by setting
   the `GOPATH` environment variable in your shell profile:

   ```
   export GOPATH=$HOME/my-go-workspace
   export PATH=$PATH:$GOPATH/bin
   ```

2. **Apply Changes**

   Reload your shell:
   ```
   source ~/.bashrc
   ```

3. **Verify**

   Check the GOPATH:
   ```
   go env GOPATH
   ```

---

3. Write and Run Your First Go Program

1. **Create a New File**

   Create a new directory and file for your Go program:
   ```
   mkdir hello-go && cd hello-go
   nano main.go
   ```

   Add the following code:
   ```go
   package main

   import "fmt"

   func main() {
       fmt.Println("Hello, World!")
   }
   ```

2. **Run the Program**

   Execute the program:
   ```
   go run main.go
   ```

   Output: Hello, World!

With these steps, you should have a fully functional Go environment on your machine!

4. Cloning the GitHub repository of the Service

1. Prerequisites

Ensure the following tools are installed on your machine:

Git: Download and install Git from the official website (https://git-scm.com/).

Verify installation by running:
```
git --version
```
Terminal or Command Prompt:
Use **Command Prompt** or **PowerShell** on Windows.
Use the **Terminal** on Linux and macOS.

---

2. Steps to Clone the Repository

Step 1: Open the Terminal/Command Prompt

Windows:
Open Command Prompt or PowerShell. Press `Win + R`, type `cmd` or `powershell`, and press Enter.

Linux/macOS:
Open the Terminal application.

Step 2: Navigate to the Desired Directory

Choose where you want to clone the repository and navigate to that directory. For example:

```
cd ~/projects
```

If the directory does not exist, create it:

```
mkdir ~/projects && cd ~/projects
```

Step 3: Clone the Repository

Run the `git clone` command with the repository URL:

```
git clone
https://github.com/priyeshkpandey/go-api-service.git
```

Step 4: Navigate to the Cloned Repository

Once cloning is complete, move into the cloned repository directory:

```
cd go-api-service
```

---

3. Verify Cloning

Check the contents of the directory to verify the repository was cloned successfully:

```
ls
```

You should see the files and folders of the `go-api-service` repository.

---

4. Additional Notes

If the repository is private, you'll need to authenticate with GitHub. Use one of the following methods:

SSH: Set up an SSH key and configure it with your GitHub account. Replace the HTTPS URL with the SSH URL:

```
git clone git@github.com:priyeshkpandey/go-api-service.git
```

Personal Access Token: When prompted for a password, use a personal access token instead. You can generate it in your GitHub account settings under "Developer settings > Personal access tokens."

By following these steps, you'll have the `go-api-service` repository cloned to your local machine, ready for use.

CHAPTER 2: Interfaces and Endpoints: The Dating App of APIs

Designing and implementing RESTful API endpoints. Learn how to make your service as user-friendly as a well-written Tinder profile.

Creating interfaces and endpoints in a microservice architecture is like planning a dinner party with your neighbors—you need clear communication to avoid chaos. Here's why they matter in GoLang:

Interfaces

In GoLang, interfaces act as contracts between components. They define what methods a type must implement without dictating how. This encourages **loose coupling** and allows for swapping implementations (like swapping chefs at your dinner party). Interfaces make your microservice code testable—mocking dependencies is easy when your code is interface-driven. Plus, if your data store or external service changes, you can update the implementation without breaking the code.

Endpoints

Endpoints are like the doorways between microservices. They allow one service to knock on another's "door" and make a request, typically using REST APIs or gRPC. Each endpoint serves a specific purpose (e.g., `/users` to manage users), ensuring modular and scalable architecture. A well-designed endpoint structure prevents services from stepping on each other's toes (no "Where's my soup?" moments).

Why Both Together?

Interfaces enable flexible, future-proof internal code, while endpoints provide a robust way for services to interact externally. Together, they ensure your microservices can evolve without turning into spaghetti (code, not dinner).

Now, let me visualize this interaction for you!

Here's a fun illustration showing how microservices interact! Each service (house) connects through endpoints (paths), with a courier delivering requests. The blueprint on top represents interfaces standardizing operations. It's all about smooth, efficient teamwork!

The Code Overview

Welcome to the whimsical world of the `go-api-service`! Imagine this repository as a bustling restaurant, where each Go file and directory plays a unique role in serving up a delightful API experience. Let's take a humorous tour through this culinary code kitchen.

1. The Head Chef: `main.go`

At the heart of our restaurant is `main.go`, the head chef orchestrating the entire operation. This file sets up the kitchen, fires up the stoves (starts the server), and ensures that all ingredients (routes and handlers) are in place. Without `main.go`, the kitchen would be in chaos, with waiters serving empty plates!

2. The Menu Planners: `controller/` **Directory**

In the `controller/` directory, we have our menu planners. They decide what dishes (endpoints) are available to the customers (clients). Each controller is like a menu section, ensuring that when a customer orders a "GET User" or a "POST User", the kitchen knows exactly what to prepare.

3. The Recipe Keepers: `service/` **Directory**

The `service/` directory houses the secret recipes. These services contain the business logic, much like recipes guide the cooking process. When a dish is ordered, the service ensures it's prepared to perfection, following the time-tested steps.

4. The Ingredient Managers: `model/` **Directory**

Every great dish starts with quality ingredients. The `model/` directory defines the data structures, akin to the ingredients used in recipes. Whether it's a User struct or a Product struct, these models ensure that the kitchen uses the right components for each dish.

5. The Pantry Organizers: `repository/` **Directory**

The `repository/` directory acts as the pantry, managing the storage and retrieval of ingredients (data). It interacts with the database, ensuring that the kitchen is always stocked and that ingredients are fetched and stored efficiently.

6. The Kitchen Helpers: `common/` **Directory**

In the `common/` directory, we find the kitchen helpers—utility functions and shared resources that assist in various tasks. From chopping vegetables (helper functions) to cleaning up (middleware), these helpers keep the kitchen running smoothly.

7. The Storage Room: `database/` **Directory**

The `database/` directory is our storage room, containing configurations and connections to the actual data storage. It's like the cellar where all the fine ingredients are kept until they're needed in the kitchen.

8. The Blueprint: `go.mod` **and** `go.sum`

These files are the architectural blueprints and inventory lists of our restaurant. They specify the dependencies and ensure that the kitchen is built with the right materials and stocked with the necessary tools.

9. The Experimental Kitchen: `test.db`

Every innovative restaurant has a test kitchen. The `test.db` file serves as a mock database, allowing chefs to experiment with new recipes without affecting the main service. It's where culinary magic is tested before hitting the main menu.

10. The Workspace Coordinator: `go.work`

The `go.work` file is like the floor manager, coordinating multiple workspaces and ensuring that all parts of the restaurant operate in harmony.

In summary, the `go-api-service` repository is a well-organized culinary establishment, where each file and directory plays a crucial role in delivering a seamless and delightful API dining experience. So, the next time you interact with this service, remember the bustling kitchen working behind the scenes to serve you the perfect data dish!

Code Implementations

Controller Package

The `controller.go` file in the `go-api-service` repository defines handlers for managing user data in a web application. It imports essential packages like `net/http` for HTTP functionalities and `encoding/json` for JSON processing.

The `GetUsers` function responds to HTTP GET requests by retrieving a list of users. It encodes the user data into JSON and writes it to the response. If encoding fails, it logs the error and sends a 500 Internal Server Error response.

The `CreateUser` function handles HTTP POST requests to add a new user. It decodes the JSON request body into a `User` struct. If decoding is successful, it appends the new user to the `users` slice and sends a 201 Created response with the user's JSON data. If decoding fails, it logs the error and sends a 400 Bad Request response.

The `UpdateUser` function manages HTTP PUT requests to update an existing user's information. It decodes the JSON request body and searches for the user by ID. If the user is found, it updates the user's details and sends a 200 OK response with the updated JSON data. If the user is not found, it sends a 404 Not Found response.

The `DeleteUser` function processes HTTP DELETE requests to remove a user by ID. It searches for the user in the `users` slice. If found, it removes the user and sends a 204 No Content response. If not, it responds with a 404 Not Found status.

In summary, this file provides CRUD (Create, Read, Update, Delete) operations for user management in the Go API service. Remember, handling user data responsibly is crucial—treat it like your morning coffee: don't spill it!

Service Package

Once upon a time in the whimsical world of Go, there existed a legendary scroll named `service.go`. This scroll was the brainchild of the grand sorcerer Priyesh K. Pandey and resided in the mystical repository known as `go-api-service`. This particular scroll was the beating heart of the Order Management Guild, orchestrating the tales of orders with finesse and flair.

The Grand Blueprint:

At the very beginning of our scroll, a proclamation is made:

```
package service
```

This declared that the scroll belonged to the esteemed `service` clan. To weave its magic, it summoned a council of trusted allies:

- The **Encoder**: Master of turning Go structures into JSON spells.
- The **IO Sage**: Guardian of data streams.
- The **HTTP Herald**: Overseer of web incantations.
- The **Mux Enchanter**: The router from the Gorilla tribe, guiding requests to their destined handlers.

Additionally, it called upon its kin:

- The **Commoner**: A shared repository of utilities.
- The **Model Artisan**: Sculptor of data structures.
- The **Repository Keeper**: Custodian of data treasures.

The OrderService Knight:

Central to our tale is the `OrderService` knight, a struct of notable repute:

```go
type OrderService struct {
    OrderRep *repository.OrderRepo
}
```

This valiant knight wielded the `OrderRep` sword, a pointer to the `OrderRepo` armory, enabling it to perform feats of data retrieval and manipulation.

Forging the Knight:

To summon an `OrderService` knight, one would invoke the `NewOrderService` spell:

```go
func NewOrderService() *OrderService {
    service := &OrderService{}
    service.OrderRep = repository.NewOrderRepo(dbFilePath)
    return service
}
```

This ritual crafted a new `OrderService` entity and equipped it with an `OrderRepo` forged from the `dbFilePath` ingot, pointing to the sacred database file `./test.db`.

The Quests Undertaken:

The `OrderService` knight embarked on several noble quests:

1. **Retrieve All Orders (`GetAllOrders`):**
   - **Objective:** Gather all existing orders.
   - **Method:** Consult the `OrderRep` to fetch the orders. If successful, present them in a JSON-encoded parchment with a 200 OK seal. If the scrolls are empty, respond with a 404 Not Found decree.
2. **Retrieve Order by ID (`GetOrder`):**
   - **Objective:** Fetch a specific order by its unique identifier.
   - **Method:** Extract the `orderId` from the path using the `Mux Enchanter`. Consult the `OrderRep` for the order. If found, display it with a 200 OK insignia; otherwise, issue a 404 Not Found proclamation.
3. **Create a New Order (`CreateOrder`):**
   - **Objective:** Add a new order to the ledger.

- ○ **Method:** Decode the incoming JSON payload into an `Order` structure. Assign it a new ID using the `common.GenerateID()` incantation. Entrust the `OrderRep` to save the order. Upon success, return the order with a 201 Created emblem.

4. **Update an Existing Order (`UpdateOrder`):**
   - ○ **Objective:** Modify the details of an existing order.
   - ○ **Method:** Extract the `orderId` and decode the JSON payload into an `Order` structure. Assign the extracted ID to the order. Command the `OrderRep` to update the order. If the order exists, confirm with a 200 OK seal; if not, declare a 404 Not Found.

5. **Delete an Order (`DeleteOrder`):**
   - ○ **Objective:** Remove an order from the records.
   - ○ **Method:** Extract the `orderId`. Instruct the `OrderRep` to delete the order. If the order was present and removed, acknowledge with a 200 OK stamp; otherwise, issue a 404 Not Found notice.

The Art of Communication:

To convey responses, the knight employed two trusted methods:

- `buildJsonResponse`: Crafted a JSON response with the appropriate status code and payload.
- `buildErrorJsonResponse`: Fashioned an error message in JSON format, detailing the error and its nature.

In Conclusion:

The `service.go` scroll stands as a testament to the harmonious blend of structure and function in the Go kingdom. Through its well-defined `OrderService` knight and its suite of quests, it ensures that the realm of order management operates seamlessly, all while adhering to the principles of clean and efficient codecraft.

CHAPTER 3 : Middleware: The Secret Sauce to Your API Burger

Implementing middleware for logging, authentication, and error handling. Because every great service needs a layer of spice!

Alright, let's make this fun! Here's a list of middleware for microservices, explained in a humorous, slightly over-the-top way:

---

1. Authentication and Authorization Middleware

Imagine this as the nightclub bouncer of your microservice.

- **What it does**: Checks IDs (tokens, credentials) at the door. No token? No entry. Token expired? Come back sober, buddy.
- **Funny twist**: It even checks if you're on the VIP list (roles/permissions) before letting you into the secret lounge.

---

2. Logging and Monitoring Middleware

Meet the diary-keeping gossip queen.

- **What it does**: Writes down every little thing that happens—every visit, every error, every suspicious look someone gave the API.
- **Funny twist**: It might even send this juicy gossip to the observability gods like Grafana and Prometheus, so they can keep an eye on your service 24/7.

---

3. Rate Limiting and Throttling Middleware

The strict parent who limits your screen time.

- **What it does**: "One request per second, young man, and that's final!" Overstep the limit? You're grounded (429 Too Many Requests).
- **Funny twist**: It doesn't care if you're Jeff Bezos or a random bot—it's fair but ruthless.

4. Request and Response Transformation Middleware

The master chef of middleware.

- **What it does**: Takes your raw JSON ingredients, chops them up, sprinkles in some headers, and serves a piping-hot, transformed response.
- **Funny twist**: It's so creative it might serve you a pineapple-on-pizza JSON, whether you like it or not.

5. Data Validation Middleware

The grammar nerd who corrects your mistakes.

- **What it does**: "Oh, your `email` field is missing an @? That's wrong!" It double-checks every field in your payload like an overzealous teacher grading homework.
- **Funny twist**: Even if you're one comma off, it'll send you home with a *400 Bad Request* red mark.

6. Error Handling Middleware

The customer service rep who stays calm during chaos.

- **What it does**: Transforms catastrophic meltdowns into polite "Oops, something went wrong" messages.
- **Funny twist**: You get a beautifully formatted error response while the service is quietly sobbing in the background.

7. Security Middleware

The paranoid security guard who sees threats everywhere.

- **What it does**: Scans your requests for anything fishy, like SQL injections or Cross-Site Scripting (XSS). It's got a panic button for anything remotely shady.
- **Funny twist**: Sometimes, it's *too* cautious. "Oh, you meant to use a single quote? Nope. Not on my watch."

8. Request Tracking and Correlation Middleware

The detective with a magnifying glass.

- **What it does**: Tags every request with a unique ID so it can track its journey across microservices like a crime-solving Sherlock Holmes.
- **Funny twist**: "Elementary, my dear developer, this request came from Service A and crashed Service C."

---

9. Cache Middleware

The lazy genius.

- **What it does**: "Why calculate the result again? I'll just remember it." Stores frequent responses in memory (like Redis) to save time and energy.
- **Funny twist**: Occasionally forgets things and has to awkwardly calculate them all over again.

---

10. Circuit Breaker Middleware

The self-preservation mechanism.

- **What it does**: When a downstream service keeps failing, it says, "Okay, no more calls to that service for now. Let's avoid burning out."
- **Funny twist**: It's like your friend who says, "Stop texting your ex; they're not replying."

---

11. Load Balancing Middleware

The traffic cop of microservices.

- **What it does**: Waves requests down the right lanes, ensuring no one server gets overwhelmed.
- **Funny twist**: It's that overly enthusiastic person at parties shouting, "Everyone gets equal snacks!"

---

12. Compression Middleware

The Marie Kondo of data.

- **What it does**: Squishes your giant payload into something smaller to "spark joy" for your network bandwidth.
- **Funny twist**: Sometimes it compresses so much, the payload comes out like, "What is this tiny blob?!" (but it works).

---

13. Localization Middleware

Your multilingual friend.

- **What it does**: Reads the client's language preferences (`Accept-Language`) and responds in their preferred tongue.
- **Funny twist**: Occasionally, it's that one friend who insists on practicing their French with everyone.

---

14. API Gateway Middleware

The concierge of your API hotel.

- **What it does**: Handles routing, load balancing, security, and even offers menu suggestions (API versions).
- **Funny twist**: "Ah, I see you're here for `/v2/orders`. Right this way, sir!"

---

15. Session Management Middleware

The babysitter of user sessions.

- **What it does**: Keeps track of which user is who, making sure everyone gets their own cookies.
- **Funny twist**: If it forgets a session, you're logged out faster than you can say, "Where did my cart go?"

---

16. Retry and Timeout Middleware

Your persistent but patient friend.

- **What it does**: "Oh, the service didn't reply? Let me try again. And again. Okay, fine, I'm done waiting!"
- **Funny twist**: It's the person who knocks on a door three times, then leaves a passive-aggressive note when no one answers.

---

17. Service Mesh Middleware

The overachiever.

- **What it does**: Handles traffic routing, observability, security, and even service discovery—basically everything you ever wanted.
- **Funny twist**: It's that one colleague who has five screens, takes perfect notes, and still finds time to hit the gym.

---

18. Analytics Middleware

The data nerd with glasses.

- **What it does**: Tracks every request, response, and user behavior, and then creates pie charts no one asked for.
- **Funny twist**: "Hey, did you know your `POST /login` API is getting 37.2% more traffic on Fridays at 3:12 PM?"

These middleware might sound quirky, but they're the unsung heroes of microservices, ensuring your systems stay functional, secure, and hilarious.

Implementing Your Middleware

Ahoy, brave developer! So, you've embarked on the quest to enhance your Go microservice, have you? Fear not, for I shall be your jester-guide, presenting you with a merry list of middleware suggestions to fortify your service's defenses and capabilities. Let the jesting commence!

---

1. The Gatekeeper (Authentication and Authorization):

Purpose: Imagine a burly bouncer at the entrance of your service, ensuring only the worthy (authenticated users) gain entry.

Suggestion: Implement JWT (JSON Web Tokens) to verify the identity of incoming requests. It's like handing out exclusive VIP badges!

---

2. The Town Crier (Logging):

Purpose: This fellow shouts out every significant event happening in your service town square, ensuring no deed goes unnoticed.

Suggestion: Integrate structured logging using libraries like Zap or Logrus. This way, every action is documented, and the tales of your service are preserved for posterity.

---

3. The Speed Enforcer (Rate Limiting):

Purpose: Think of this as the strict constable ensuring no one overwhelms your service by sending too many requests in a short span—no speeding in this town!

Suggestion: Use middleware to limit the number of requests a user can make, preventing any single user from hogging all the resources.

---

4. The Translator (Request and Response Transformation):

Purpose: This clever chap ensures that all incoming and outgoing messages are in a language (format) that both your service and its clients understand.

Suggestion: Implement middleware to transform request payloads and response bodies as needed, ensuring seamless communication.

---

5. The Bodyguard (Security):

Purpose: Standing ever vigilant, this protector defends your service against malicious attacks and nefarious deeds.

Suggestion: Employ middleware to handle CORS, input sanitization, and other security measures, keeping the bad actors at bay.

6. The Gossip (Request Logging):

Purpose: This nosy neighbor keeps track of every visitor, noting down who came, what they did, and when they left.

Suggestion: Use middleware to log details of each request and response, aiding in monitoring and debugging.

7. The Juggler (Load Balancing):

Purpose: Expertly balancing multiple tasks, this performer ensures that no single part of your service is overwhelmed.

Suggestion: Implement load balancing to distribute incoming requests evenly across multiple instances of your service.

8. The Archivist (Caching):

Purpose: This wise keeper stores copies of frequently requested data, delivering them swiftly without bothering the main service.

Suggestion: Use caching mechanisms to store and serve common responses quickly, reducing the load on your service.

9. The Circuit Breaker (Fault Tolerance):

Purpose: Like a safety switch, this mechanism prevents your service from repeatedly trying to perform a failing operation, avoiding further damage.

Suggestion: Implement a circuit breaker pattern to gracefully handle failures and prevent cascading issues in your microservices architecture.

10. The Timekeeper (Timeouts):

Purpose: This punctual fellow ensures that no operation takes longer than it should, maintaining the rhythm of your service.

By enlisting these colorful characters into your microservice's court, you'll create a robust, efficient, and secure system that can handle the challenges of the digital realm with grace and aplomb. Onward, noble developer, to middleware glory!

CHAPTER 4 : Goroutines: More Go, Less Wait

Adding concurrency to your service with Goroutines and channels. Turning your API into a multi-tasking wizard without the caffeine jitters.

Alright, let's dive into the quirky world of **goroutines and channels** in Go, but with a fun twist and some diagrams that will make you giggle and understand simultaneously!

The World of Goroutines: The Tiny Workers

Imagine you're the CEO of a bustling factory, and you've got tons of tasks to complete. You could hire one single worker (a boring old thread) and expect them to finish everything, but why not hire **goroutines**, tiny, super-efficient workers who don't demand much?

What's a Goroutine?

Think of a goroutine as a hyperactive, multitasking minion from "Despicable Me."
You give them a task (`go doSomething()`) and off they run, buzzing around like, "Task? On it, boss!" They're lightweight, so you can spawn thousands of them without the factory floor collapsing.

Here's how it looks in Go:

```go
go fetchDataFromAPI()
go processLargeFile()
go annoyYourBoss()
```

Quirky Diagram: Goroutines in Action

```
Main Goroutine (CEO)
       |
       +-----------------+----------------+------------+
       |                 |                |            |
   [fetch data]    [process file]  [brew coffee]  [pet the dog]
```

The CEO (main goroutine) delegates tasks to the workers and goes back to sipping coffee.

Channels: The Conveyor Belt

Now, you've got all these hyperactive goroutines running around, but how do they communicate? They need something reliable to pass messages around—enter **channels**, the conveyor belt of your factory.

What's a Channel?

A channel is a magical pipe where goroutines can send and receive messages. Think of it like one worker placing a shiny new widget on the belt (`ch <- widget`), and another grabbing it (`widget := <-ch`) at the other end. It's like a factory dance party where everything flows perfectly... until someone forgets to use synchronization (oops).

Here's an example:

```go
ch := make(chan string)

// Worker 1 (Goroutine)
go func() {
    ch <- "Hello from Goroutine 1!"
}()

// Worker 2 (Goroutine)
go func() {
    message := <-ch
    fmt.Println(message)
}()
```

Quirky Diagram: Channels in Action

```
Worker 1 (Producer) --> [Channel Conveyor Belt] --> Worker 2
(Consumer)
```

Synchronous vs Asynchronous: Conveyor Belt Types

1.   **Buffered Channels**: Imagine a conveyor belt with baskets. Workers can place items on the belt, even if no one's picking them up immediately. Pretty handy!

```go
ch := make(chan int, 5) // Can hold 5 items
ch <- 42 // Drop it and forget about it
```

2.   **Unbuffered Channels**: No baskets, just direct handshakes. A worker has to wait until the other worker shows up to take the widget.

```go
ch := make(chan int) // No storage
go func() { ch <- 42 }()
fmt.Println(<-ch) // "42" is handed off directly
```

Quirky Diagram: Channel Types

```
Unbuffered:  Worker 1 --> [Conveyor] --> Worker 2
Buffered:    Worker 1 --> [Conveyor Box | Box | Box] -->
Worker 2
```

Select Statement: The Traffic Cop

When you have multiple channels, who decides which one gets processed first? Meet **select**, the traffic cop of channels. It stands in the middle of a busy intersection, yelling, "Alright, you! Your turn now!"

```go
select {
case msg := <-ch1:
    fmt.Println("Got from ch1:", msg)
case msg := <-ch2:
    fmt.Println("Got from ch2:", msg)
default:
    fmt.Println("No activity.")
}
```

Final Quirky Diagram: Goroutines + Channels

```
Main Goroutine (CEO)
    |
    +-------[ Task 1 ] <-> Channel 1 <-> Worker 1
    +-------[ Task 2 ] <-> Channel 2 <-> Worker 2
    +-------[ Task 3 ] <-> Channel 3 <-> Worker 3
```

Wrap-Up

In summary:

- **Goroutines** are like minions—efficient, lightweight workers doing tasks simultaneously.
- **Channels** are their conveyor belts, letting them pass messages and keep things orderly.
- Together, they make Go's concurrency feel like a dance party where everyone has their part to play. Just don't forget to keep track of all those minions—if you don't handle synchronization properly, your factory could descend into chaos!

Implementing Concurrency for the Service

In the whimsical realm of Go, the `service.go` file from the `go-api-service` repository is like a bustling café, serving up delightful data dishes to its patrons. However, in this particular establishment, the chefs (functions) have chosen a more traditional approach, opting not to employ the energetic waitstaff known as goroutines.

The Café Layout:

At the heart of this café is the `OrderService` struct, which acts as the maître d', coordinating orders and ensuring everything runs smoothly.

```go
type OrderService struct {
    OrderRep *repository.OrderRepo
}
```

The Menu Offerings:

The café offers a variety of services to its patrons:

- **GetAllOrders**: Presents a full menu of all available orders.
- **GetOrder**: Fetches a specific order upon request.
- **CreateOrder**: Adds a new delicacy to the menu.
- **UpdateOrder**: Modifies an existing menu item.
- **DeleteOrder**: Removes an item from the menu.

Each of these services is handled synchronously, meaning the chef prepares each dish one at a time, ensuring meticulous attention to detail.

A Peek into the Kitchen:

Let's take a closer look at the GetAllOrders function:

```go
func (service *OrderService) GetAllOrders(w
http.ResponseWriter, r *http.Request) {
    orders, err := service.OrderRep.GetAllOrders()
    if err != nil {
        buildErrorJsonResponse(w,
http.StatusInternalServerError, "Error fetching orders")
        return
    }
    if len(orders) == 0 {
        buildErrorJsonResponse(w, http.StatusNotFound, "No
orders found")
        return
    }
    buildJsonResponse(w, http.StatusOK, orders)
}
```

In this function, the chef retrieves all orders from the pantry (repository) and serves them to the customer. If there are no orders or an error occurs, the chef politely informs the patron.

Imagining Goroutines in the Café:

Now, let's envision a scenario where the café decides to hire goroutines as waitstaff. Each goroutine would handle customer requests concurrently, allowing multiple patrons to be served simultaneously. This would be akin to having a fleet of energetic servers attending to different tables at the same time, significantly increasing the café's efficiency during peak hours.

Implementing Goroutines:

To implement goroutines in the GetAllOrders function, the café could set up a channel to handle incoming orders and spawn a goroutine for each request:

```go
func (service *OrderService) GetAllOrders(w
http.ResponseWriter, r *http.Request) {
    ordersChan := make(chan []model.Order)
    errorChan := make(chan error)
```

```go
go func() {
    orders, err := service.OrderRep.GetAllOrders()
    if err != nil {
        errorChan <- err
        return
    }
    ordersChan <- orders
}()

select {
case orders := <-ordersChan:
    if len(orders) == 0 {
        buildErrorJsonResponse(w, http.StatusNotFound, "No
orders found")
        return
    }
    buildJsonResponse(w, http.StatusOK, orders)
case err := <-errorChan:
    buildErrorJsonResponse(w,
http.StatusInternalServerError, "Error fetching orders")
    }
}
```

In this setup, the café assigns a goroutine to fetch orders, allowing the main function to handle other tasks concurrently. This approach can improve response times and overall efficiency, especially during busy periods.

Conclusion:

While the current implementation of `service.go` operates synchronously, introducing goroutines could transform the café into a more dynamic and efficient establishment. However, it's essential to manage these goroutines carefully to ensure that orders are processed correctly and resources are utilized effectively.

CHAPTER 5 : Testing: The Art of Breaking Your Own Stuff

Writing unit tests, mocking, and integration tests. A survival guide to catching bugs before your users do (and saving yourself from public shame).

Alright, let's dive into writing some Go tests for the API endpoints in the `controller.go` file, but in a way that makes testing feel like a delightful comedy skit. Here's how our test "adventure" unfolds:

Meet the Cast: API Endpoints

The API is like a group of quirky friends, each with their own personality:

1. `getAllOrders`: The helpful one who knows *everything* about all the orders.
2. `getOrder`: The snoop who can fetch one specific order like a gossip-loving detective.
3. `createOrder`: The dreamer who brings new orders into existence.
4. `updateOrder`: The perfectionist who likes tweaking and updating details.
5. `deleteOrder`: The executioner who makes orders vanish with a snap (RIP).

Now, let's write tests to make sure each character is doing their job without slacking off!

Setting the Stage

Before jumping in, we need:

- **Fake Requests:** Like prank calls, but they're productive.
- **Fake Recorders:** To eavesdrop on what the endpoint says in response.
- **Mock Data:** So no real database is harmed during the testing chaos.

Test 1: The Know-It-All (`getAllOrders`)

This is the endpoint that brags about knowing every order. Let's test if it's telling the truth!

```go
func TestGetAllOrders(t *testing.T) {

    // Set up the prank call

    req, err := http.NewRequest("GET", "/orders", nil)

    if err != nil {

        t.Fatal("Failed to create request:", err)

    }


    // Record the gossip

    rr := httptest.NewRecorder()

    handler := http.HandlerFunc(getAllOrders)


    // Ring, ring! The endpoint picks up.

    handler.ServeHTTP(rr, req)


    // Did it deliver?

    if status := rr.Code; status != http.StatusOK {

        t.Errorf("getAllOrders failed! Got status %v, wanted
%v", status, http.StatusOK)

    }


    // Check if it spilled all the orders
```

```go
    if len(rr.Body.String()) == 0 {

        t.Error("getAllOrders is keeping secrets! Expected
some data, got none.")

    }

}
```

Test 2: The Detective (`getOrder`)

This snoopy endpoint fetches a specific order by ID. Let's make sure it's not snoozing on the job.

```go
func TestGetOrder(t *testing.T) {

    // Create a fake order ID

    orderID := "123"


    // Set up the detective's snoop request

    req, err := http.NewRequest("GET", "/orders/"+orderID,
nil)

    if err != nil {

        t.Fatal("Failed to create request:", err)

    }


    // Simulate the URL variable for order ID

    req = mux.SetURLVars(req, map[string]string{"id":
orderID})
```

```go
	// Record the detective's findings

	rr := httptest.NewRecorder()

	handler := http.HandlerFunc(getOrder)


	// Knock, knock! Detective at the door.

	handler.ServeHTTP(rr, req)


	// Did the detective show up?

	if status := rr.Code; status != http.StatusOK {

		t.Errorf("getOrder failed to find the order! Got
status %v, wanted %v", status, http.StatusOK)

	}


	// Did it find the right order?

	if !strings.Contains(rr.Body.String(), orderID) {

		t.Errorf("getOrder fetched the wrong gossip! Expected
order ID %v in response, but got %v", orderID,
rr.Body.String())

	}

}
```

Test 3: The Dreamer (`createOrder`)

This endpoint loves to create new orders, but is it actually doing its job?

```go
func TestCreateOrder(t *testing.T) {

    // Dream up a new order

    newOrder := `{"item": "Magic Wand", "quantity": 1}`

    req, err := http.NewRequest("POST", "/orders",
strings.NewReader(newOrder))

    if err != nil {

        t.Fatal("Failed to create request:", err)

    }

    req.Header.Set("Content-Type", "application/json")


    // Record the dream

    rr := httptest.NewRecorder()

    handler := http.HandlerFunc(createOrder)


    // Tell the endpoint to make it happen

    handler.ServeHTTP(rr, req)


    // Did the dream come true?

    if status := rr.Code; status != http.StatusCreated {

        t.Errorf("createOrder failed! Got status %v, wanted
%v", status, http.StatusCreated)
```

```go
    }

    // Check if the new order is in the response

    if !strings.Contains(rr.Body.String(), "Magic Wand") {

        t.Error("createOrder missed the magic! Expected the
item in the response but got nothing magical.")

    }

}
```

Test 4: The Perfectionist (`updateOrder`)

The perfectionist loves to update details. Let's make sure it's actually updating the right
stuff.

```go
func TestUpdateOrder(t *testing.T) {

    // Fake the updated order details

    updatedOrder := `{"item": "Enchanted Sword", "quantity":
2}`

    orderID := "123"

    req, err := http.NewRequest("PUT", "/orders/"+orderID,
strings.NewReader(updatedOrder))

    if err != nil {

        t.Fatal("Failed to create request:", err)

    }

    req.Header.Set("Content-Type", "application/json")
```

```go
	req = mux.SetURLVars(req, map[string]string{"id":
orderID})

	// Record the update process

	rr := httptest.NewRecorder()

	handler := http.HandlerFunc(updateOrder)


	// "Perfect it!" says the endpoint

	handler.ServeHTTP(rr, req)


	// Did it go through?

	if status := rr.Code; status != http.StatusOK {

		t.Errorf("updateOrder messed up! Got status %v, wanted
%v", status, http.StatusOK)

	}


	// Check if it's been perfected

	if !strings.Contains(rr.Body.String(), "Enchanted Sword")
{

		t.Error("updateOrder forgot the enchanted details!
Expected updated item in the response.")

	}

}
```

Test 5: The Executioner (`deleteOrder`)

The executioner takes no prisoners. Let's test if it's doing its job with precision.

```go
func TestDeleteOrder(t *testing.T) {

    // Target an order for execution

    orderID := "123"

    req, err := http.NewRequest("DELETE", "/orders/"+orderID,
nil)

    if err != nil {

        t.Fatal("Failed to create request:", err)

    }

    req = mux.SetURLVars(req, map[string]string{"id":
orderID})


    // Record the disappearance

    rr := httptest.NewRecorder()

    handler := http.HandlerFunc(deleteOrder)


    // Snap! The order is gone.

    handler.ServeHTTP(rr, req)


    // Did the execution happen?

    if status := rr.Code; status != http.StatusNoContent {

        t.Errorf("deleteOrder botched it! Got status %v,
wanted %v", status, http.StatusNoContent)
```

```
        }
    }
```


The Curtain Call

There you have it! These tests make sure every endpoint is pulling its weight and acting like the character they're meant to be. Whether it's gossiping, dreaming, perfecting, or vanishing orders, your API is now thoroughly inspected—and hilariously so!

CHAPTER 6 : Database, or: How I Learned to Stop Worrying and Love SQL

Connecting your service to a database and managing migrations. No more sleepless nights wondering where your data went.

Alright, buckle up, because we're about to embark on a Go adventure to connect to multiple databases in a **loosely coupled, highly entertaining** manner! Picture your databases as quirky characters from a sitcom, each with its own personality, and your Go code as the peacekeeper who knows how to talk to all of them. Let's dive in:

The Problem:

You've got a bunch of databases—PostgreSQL (the strict professor), MySQL (the laid-back artist), MongoDB (the hipster who doesn't believe in structure), and Redis (the overachieving intern). How do you connect to all of them without making your code a tangled mess? Simple! You use **interfaces** and **factory patterns** to keep things loosely coupled.

Step 1: Define an Interface

First, we need a universal "language" that all databases can understand. Think of it as a mediator between the databases and your Go code.

```go
// Database is our universal language (interface)

type Database interface {

    Connect() error

    Query(query string) (string, error)

    Close() error

}
```

Step 2: Write Structs for Each Database

Now, let's give each database its personality by creating structs that implement the Database interface.

PostgreSQL: The Strict Professor

```go
type PostgresDB struct{}


func (p *PostgresDB) Connect() error {

    fmt.Println("PostgresDB: Connecting to the database with
strict credentials...")

    return nil

}



func (p *PostgresDB) Query(query string) (string, error) {

    fmt.Printf("PostgresDB: Executing query with precision:
%s\n", query)

    return "Postgres result", nil

}



func (p *PostgresDB) Close() error {

    fmt.Println("PostgresDB: Closing connection. Don't forget
your assignments!")

    return nil

}
```

MySQL: The Laid-Back Artist

```go
type MySQLDB struct{}


func (m *MySQLDB) Connect() error {

    fmt.Println("MySQLDB: Yo, connecting to the database. Take
it easy!")

    return nil

}




func (m *MySQLDB) Query(query string) (string, error) {

    fmt.Printf("MySQLDB: Running this masterpiece of a query:
%s\n", query)

    return "MySQL result", nil

}




func (m *MySQLDB) Close() error {

    fmt.Println("MySQLDB: Connection closed. Time for a coffee
break.")

    return nil

}
```

MongoDB: The Hipster


```go
type MongoDB struct{}



func (m *MongoDB) Connect() error {

    fmt.Println("MongoDB: Connecting... No schema? No problem,
man!")

    return nil

}



func (m *MongoDB) Query(query string) (string, error) {

    fmt.Printf("MongoDB: Searching through my unstructured
vibes: %s\n", query)

    return "Mongo result", nil

}



func (m *MongoDB) Close() error {

    fmt.Println("MongoDB: Closing connection. Keep it cool.")

    return nil

}
```

Redis: The Overachieving Intern

```go
type RedisDB struct{}


func (r *RedisDB) Connect() error {

    fmt.Println("RedisDB: Connecting super-fast. Ready for
action!")

    return nil

}



func (r *RedisDB) Query(query string) (string, error) {

    fmt.Printf("RedisDB: Looking up cache for query: %s\n",
query)

    return "Redis result", nil

}



func (r *RedisDB) Close() error {

    fmt.Println("RedisDB: Done already? I'll keep working in
the background.")

    return nil

}
```

Step 3: Create a Factory

Here's the mastermind of our sitcom, the one who decides which database to talk to based on a simple request.

```go
func DatabaseFactory(dbType string) (Database, error) {

    switch dbType {

    case "postgres":

        return &PostgresDB{}, nil

    case "mysql":

        return &MySQLDB{}, nil

    case "mongo":

        return &MongoDB{}, nil

    case "redis":

        return &RedisDB{}, nil

    default:

        return nil, fmt.Errorf("Unknown database type: %s",
    dbType)

    }

}
```

Step 4: Use the Factory in Your Code

Now, the fun part! Let's use our factory to connect to different databases dynamically. Here's what your sitcom scene might look like:

```go
func main() {

    // Choose your database character

    dbType := "mongo" // Try "postgres", "mysql", "redis", etc.

    database, err := DatabaseFactory(dbType)

    if err != nil {

        fmt.Printf("Error: %v\n", err)

        return

    }


    // Let's interact with the database

    err = database.Connect()

    if err != nil {

        fmt.Printf("Error connecting to %s: %v\n", dbType, err)

        return

    }


    result, err := database.Query("SELECT * FROM sitcom_characters")

    if err != nil {
```

```go
        fmt.Printf("Error querying %s: %v\n", dbType, err)

        return

    }

    fmt.Printf("Query Result from %s: %s\n", dbType, result)


    // Close the connection

    err = database.Close()

    if err != nil {

        fmt.Printf("Error closing connection to %s: %v\n",
dbType, err)

    }

}
```

What Happens When You Run This?

Let's say you set `dbType := "postgres"`. The output might look something like this:

```
PostgresDB: Connecting to the database with strict
credentials...

PostgresDB: Executing query with precision: SELECT * FROM
sitcom_characters

Query Result from postgres: Postgres result

PostgresDB: Closing connection. Don't forget your assignments!
```

Switch it to `dbType := "redis"`:

```
RedisDB: Connecting super-fast. Ready for action!

RedisDB: Looking up cache for query: SELECT * FROM
sitcom_characters

Query Result from redis: Redis result

RedisDB: Done already? I'll keep working in the background.
```

Why Is This Awesome?

1. **Loosely Coupled**: Each database character is independent. You can add or change them without touching the rest of the code.
2. **Dynamic**: Want to switch databases? Just change the `dbType`—no refactoring required!
3. **Funny Personalities**: Your databases come alive with their own quirks. (Bonus: Makes debugging less soul-crushing!)

And there you have it—a sitcom-style, loosely coupled database connection system in Go! Now, go forth and make your databases part of the comedy cast of your application.

CHAPTER 7 : Deployment: Ship It Like You Mean It

Dockerizing the app and deploying it using tools like Kubernetes or a cloud platform. Because nothing says success like yelling "It works on my machine!" while your server crashes.

Alright, buckle up, because we're about to embark on a *comical* journey to Dockerize your Go microservice and unleash it into the wild using Kubernetes. It's like turning your tiny Go minion into a superhero, giving it a cape (container) and a fortress (Kubernetes cluster). Let's dive in!

Step 1: Wrapping Your Go Service in a Docker Cape

First, we'll slap a Docker cape on your Go microservice to give it superpowers.

The Dockerfile: The Hero's Outfit

Imagine the Dockerfile as the superhero's costume—it's lightweight, snazzy, and helps your service fight crime (or at least run efficiently).

```
# Stage 1: Build the Go application

FROM golang:1.20 AS builder


# Set the working directory inside the container

WORKDIR /app


# Copy the Go module files and download dependencies

COPY go.mod go.sum ./

RUN go mod download


# Copy the rest of the app code into the container
```

```dockerfile
COPY . .

# Build the application into a binary called "service"
RUN go build -o service


# Stage 2: Create a minimal runtime image
FROM alpine:latest


# Copy the binary from the builder stage
COPY --from=builder /app/service /service


# Expose the port your service listens on
EXPOSE 8080


# Command to run your Go service
CMD ["/service"]
```

What's Happening?

1. **Stage 1 (Builder)**: Think of this as the hero training montage. We download dependencies, compile the Go code, and emerge with a shiny binary (`service`).
2. **Stage 2 (Runtime)**: This is where our hero dons the lightweight alpine suit (a minimalist image) and prepares for action.

Build Your Container

Run this magical command to wrap your service in its Docker cape:

```
docker build -t go-microservice:v1
```

Boom! Your service is now Dockerized and ready to strut its stuff.

Step 2: Running the Container Locally

Before throwing your hero into battle, test it locally to make sure it works:

```
docker run -p 8080:8080 go-microservice:v1
```

Visit `http://localhost:8080`, and if your service responds, it's like hearing the crowd cheer: "Our hero is ready!"

Step 3: Deploying the Hero in Kubernetes

Now it's time to send your containerized hero into the Kubernetes universe, where it can join forces with other microservices and save the world (or just serve HTTP requests).

Kubernetes YAML Files: The Hero's Guidebook

You'll need three YAML files to guide your hero:

1. **Deployment (Where the hero resides)**
2. **Service (How the hero connects with the world)**
3. **Namespace (The hero's kingdom)**

---

1. Deployment YAML

Here's where you tell Kubernetes how to run your containerized superhero:

```yaml
apiVersion: apps/v1

kind: Deployment

metadata:

  name: go-microservice

  labels:

    app: go-microservice

spec:

  replicas: 3 # Three heroes for redundancy-because even
superheroes need backups!

  selector:

    matchLabels:

      app: go-microservice

  template:

    metadata:

      labels:

        app: go-microservice

    spec:

      containers:

      - name: go-microservice

        image: go-microservice:v1 # Our Dockerized hero!

        ports:
```

```
          - containerPort: 8080
```


---

2. Service YAML

This is the superhero hotline—how the outside world reaches your hero:

```
apiVersion: v1

kind: Service

metadata:

  name: go-microservice

spec:

  selector:

    app: go-microservice

  ports:

    - protocol: TCP

      port: 80 # External hotline

      targetPort: 8080 # The port your hero listens on

  type: LoadBalancer # To get a public IP
```

---

3. Namespace YAML

Every superhero needs a secret base. Let's give your service its own namespace:

```yaml
apiVersion: v1

kind: Namespace

metadata:

  name: hero-namespace
```

Step 4: Deploy the YAML Files

Now, let's send your superhero into the Kubernetes galaxy!

1. **Create the namespace:**
   ```
   kubectl apply -f namespace.yaml
   ```
2. **Deploy the service and deployment:**
   ```
   kubectl apply -f deployment.yaml -n hero-namespace

   kubectl apply -f service.yaml -n hero-namespace
   ```

Step 5: Verify the Deployment

Run these commands to make sure your hero is alive and kicking:

- **Check the pods (superhero clones):**
   ```
   kubectl get pods -n hero-namespace
   ```
- **Check the service (superhero hotline):**
   ```
   kubectl get service -n hero-namespace
   ```

If everything's running, congrats! Your superhero is out there saving the (microservice) world.

Step 6: Test the Service

Get the external IP of your service:

```
kubectl get service go-microservice -n hero-namespace
```

Now, visit the IP in your browser or use `curl`:

```
curl http://<EXTERNAL-IP>
```

If your service responds, it's like hearing your superhero say, "I'm here to help!"

The Comical Wrap-Up

Here's a summary of our superhero journey:

1. **Dockerized the Go service**: We gave our microservice a cool Docker cape.
2. **Tested locally**: Because even superheroes need rehearsals.
3. **Deployed to Kubernetes**: Built a kingdom (namespace), deployed the hero (deployment), and gave it a hotline (service).
4. **Verified and tested**: Ensured our hero is actually out there, saving the world one HTTP request at a time.

So now your Go microservice is not just a codebase—it's a superhero, equipped to handle requests, fight bugs, and scale heroically across the Kubernetes universe.

CHAPTER 8 : Monitoring: Keeping an Eye on Your Franken-App

Setting up monitoring, logging, and metrics with tools like Prometheus and Grafana. Be the all-seeing eye of Sauron, but for uptime instead of doom.

Alright, traveler, let us embark on an epic journey to implement **monitoring for a microservice in Go**, all while channeling the spirit of Middle-earth. Imagine your microservice as Frodo, bravely venturing through the unpredictable lands of production, where dangers lurk, and only vigilant monitoring (a.k.a Gandalf) can guide it to safety. Let's begin!

Step 1: The Fellowship of the Metrics

Every great quest begins with assembling a fellowship. In this case, you'll need:

1. **Prometheus**: The all-seeing Eye of Gondor (not Mordor, don't confuse them).
2. **Grafana**: The Elven craftsman of dashboards—elegant and powerful.
3. **Your Microservice**: Frodo the Brave, tasked with carrying the responsibility of responding to requests… while being observed.

Step 2: Embedding Monitoring in Your Go Service

Your microservice needs the ability to *speak* its health, performance, and requests. To do this, we'll gift it the magical **Prometheus client library** (`github.com/prometheus/client_golang/prometheus`)—kind of like Frodo getting Sting.

Install the Prometheus Library:

First, arm your service with the Prometheus library:

```
go get github.com/prometheus/client_golang/prometheus

go get github.com/prometheus/client_golang/prometheus/promhttp
```

Define the Metrics:

Metrics are like the records in the Red Book of Westmarch—valuable information about your microservice's journey. Here's what you'll measure:

1. **Request Counts**: How many travelers (requests) visited?
2. **Request Duration**: Did the journey take seconds… or an eternity?
3. **Errors**: Did Orcs (bugs) cause trouble?

```go
package main


import (

    "net/http"

    "github.com/prometheus/client_golang/prometheus"

    "github.com/prometheus/client_golang/prometheus/promhttp"

)



// Declare the metrics (our gifts from the Valar)

var (

    requestCount = prometheus.NewCounterVec(

        prometheus.CounterOpts{

            Name: "requests_total",

            Help: "Number of HTTP requests processed",

        },

        []string{"method", "endpoint"},

    )

    requestDuration = prometheus.NewHistogramVec(
```

```go
        prometheus.HistogramOpts{

            Name:     "request_duration_seconds",

            Help:     "Time taken to process requests",

            Buckets: prometheus.DefBuckets, // Gandalf-level
wisdom here

        },

        []string{"method", "endpoint"},

    )

)


func init() {

    // Register the metrics with Prometheus

    prometheus.MustRegister(requestCount)

    prometheus.MustRegister(requestDuration)

}
```

Wrap the Metrics Around the Service:

Your Frodo (microservice) needs a cloak of monitoring to shield it during its treacherous journey. Let's write middleware to record metrics:

```go
func monitor(next http.Handler) http.Handler {

    return http.HandlerFunc(func(w http.ResponseWriter, r
*http.Request) {

        endpoint := r.URL.Path

        method := r.Method



        // Start tracking time

        timer :=
prometheus.NewTimer(requestDuration.WithLabelValues(method,
endpoint))

        defer timer.ObserveDuration()



        // Increment request count

        requestCount.WithLabelValues(method, endpoint).Inc()



        // Pass the call to the actual handler

        next.ServeHTTP(w, r)

    })

}
```

Expose the Metrics Endpoint:

Every hero needs a scribe to tell their tale. The `/metrics` endpoint will let Prometheus collect your service's metrics like Sam writing Frodo's story.

```go
func main() {

    mux := http.NewServeMux()


    // Your real endpoint

    mux.Handle("/hello", monitor(http.HandlerFunc(func(w
http.ResponseWriter, r *http.Request) {

        w.Write([]byte("Hello, Middle-earth!"))

    })))


    // The metrics endpoint

    mux.Handle("/metrics", promhttp.Handler())


    // Start the service

    http.ListenAndServe(":8080", mux)

}
```

Now, when you visit `http://localhost:8080/metrics`, you'll see a magical text dump of your service's journey stats.

Step 3: Prometheus: The Watcher on the Wall

Prometheus is like Gandalf—watching over your service, recording every step of its journey, and blowing a horn when things go wrong.

Prometheus Configuration:

Here's a `prometheus.yml` file to guide Gandalf's gaze:

```yaml
global:

  scrape_interval: 15s # Gandalf checks in every 15 seconds


scrape_configs:

  - job_name: "go-microservice"

    static_configs:

      - targets: ["localhost:8080"] # Where Frodo's metrics
are exposed
```

Run Prometheus:

```
prometheus --config.file=prometheus.yml
```

Visit Prometheus at `http://localhost:9090` to see the data Gandalf has gathered.

Step 4: Grafana: The Elven Dashboard

Grafana is like Galadriel—beautiful, insightful, and capable of crafting dashboards that light up like the Phial of Eärendil.

Set Up Grafana:

1. Download and run Grafana:
   ```
   docker run -d -p 3000:3000 grafana/grafana
   ```
2. Log in at http://localhost:3000 (default username/password: admin/admin).
3. Add Prometheus as a data source (use http://localhost:9090).

Create a Dashboard:

- Create a new panel.
- Query metrics like:
    - requests_total (to see how many visitors Frodo has had).
    - request_duration_seconds (to monitor the time it takes to respond).
    - errors_total (to track when Frodo trips over Orcs).

Step 5: Alerts: The Horn of Gondor

Sometimes, things go wrong. Your service might face an attack (too many errors) or become sluggish. Prometheus can sound the **Horn of Gondor** (alerts) when trouble arises.

Define Alerts in Prometheus:

Add an alert to the prometheus.yml file:

```
alerting:

  alertmanagers:

    - static_configs:

        - targets: ["localhost:9093"]


  rule_files:
```

```yaml
  - "alerts.yml"
```

Create `alerts.yml` for an alert like:

```yaml
groups:
  - name: service-alerts
    rules:
      - alert: TooManyErrors
        expr: requests_total{endpoint="/hello", method="GET"} > 100
        for: 1m
        labels:
          severity: critical
        annotations:
          summary: "Frodo is overwhelmed!"
          description: "Too many requests for Frodo to handle. Check your service."
```

The Final Act: A Safe Frodo

With Prometheus (Gandalf) monitoring and Grafana (Galadriel) showing the way, Frodo (your microservice) is no longer alone in its quest. It's now equipped to handle the treacherous paths of production, while you, the wise Lord of the Microservices, sit back with a cup of tea, watching your dashboards light up like fireworks at Bilbo's birthday party.

"You shall not pass… unnoticed!"

Before you Go

Ah, so you've decided to embark on the glorious adventure of contributing code to
`https://github.com/priyeshkpandey/go-api-service`? Fear not, noble coder!
Here's a **step-by-step guide** to creating a Pull Request (PR) with the charm of a tale from
Middle-earth.

Step 1: Fork the Repository (Your Own Shire)

You're Frodo, and the repository is the One Ring. To begin your journey, you need to **fork
the repo** to create your own version.

1. **Go to the repository**: https://github.com/priyeshkpandey/go-api-service.
2. In the top-right corner, click **Fork** (it's the button with a tiny wizard's wand).
3. Now you have your very own copy of the repository in your GitHub account! This
   is your Shire—safe and sound to experiment with.

Step 2: Clone the Fork (Bring the Ring Home)

Now that you've got your own copy, it's time to bring it to your local machine (your cozy
Hobbit hole).

```
# Replace 'your-username' with your GitHub username

git clone https://github.com/your-username/go-api-service.git

cd go-api-service
```

This downloads the code to your local machine so you can start working on it.

Step 3: Create a New Branch (Form Your Fellowship)

It's never wise to directly work on the `main` branch. Instead, create a new branch for your specific task. Think of it as forming a fellowship for your mission.

```
git checkout -b feature/add-awesome-feature
```

Here's the naming convention:

- `feature/` for adding new features.
- `bugfix/` for fixing bugs.
- `chore/` for non-code changes like documentation updates.

Step 4: Make Your Changes (Begin Your Journey)

Now, it's time to wield your coding sword and make some magic happen! Open the project in your favorite code editor (like VS Code), and add your changes.

For example:

- Add a new API endpoint.
- Fix a bug in the existing code.
- Update the README with better instructions.

Test your code thoroughly, because, as Gandalf once said: *"A single bug can ruin the fate of Middle-earth."*

Step 5: Commit Your Changes (Document Your Tale)

Once your changes are ready, commit them with a meaningful message. This is like chronicling your journey in the Red Book of Westmarch.

```
git add .

git commit -m "Add a new feature for handling XYZ"
```

Step 6: Push Your Changes (Send Ravens to Gondor)

Now, send your branch back to your forked repository on GitHub:

```
git push origin feature/add-awesome-feature
```

This pushes your changes to the `feature/add-awesome-feature` branch in your forked repo.

Step 7: Create a Pull Request (Request the Council)

Now comes the exciting part—asking the project maintainers (the Council of Elrond) to review and merge your changes.

1. Go to **your forked repo** on GitHub.
2. You'll see a "Compare & pull request" button. Click it.
3. Fill in the PR details:
    - **Title**: Be descriptive (e.g., "Add feature to handle API rate limiting").
    - **Description**: Explain what you did, why you did it, and how it helps the project. If you fixed a bug, mention the issue number if it exists (e.g., "Fixes #42").
4. Click **Create Pull Request**.

Step 8: Wait for Review (The Council Decides)

The maintainers (possibly Priyesh himself) will review your PR. Be prepared for:

- **Feedback**: They might ask for changes. This is normal—think of it as Gandalf's wise counsel!
- **Approval**: Once they're satisfied, they'll merge your PR into the main branch, making you a proud contributor.

Step 9: Sync Your Fork (Stay Up to Date)

After your PR is merged (or if the original repo gets updated), keep your fork in sync with the original repo to avoid falling behind.

```
git remote add upstream
https://github.com/priyeshkpandey/go-api-service.git

git fetch upstream

git merge upstream/main
```

Step 10: Celebrate!

You've successfully contributed to the **go-api-service** project! Pour yourself a pint at the Green Dragon Inn and celebrate like a true Hobbit.

Final Advice from Gandalf

- **Be Respectful**: Follow the project's contribution guidelines, if they exist.
- **Write Clean Code**: Ensure your code is readable and tested.
- **Document Your Work**: Update comments and documentation if needed.

Remember, *"Even the smallest contribution can change the course of the project."*

www.ingramcontent.com/pod-product-compliance
Lightning Source LLC
Chambersburg PA
CBHW040216110726
48005CB00019B/3043